THE
BROWN RICE
COOKBOOK

C0-AME-161

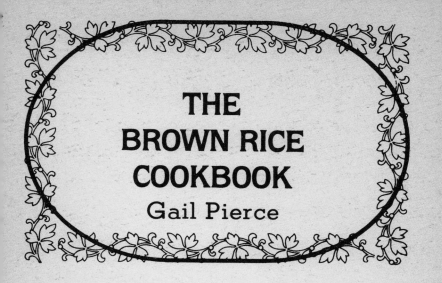

THE
BROWN RICE
COOKBOOK

Gail Pierce

A COMET BOOK
Published by the Paperback Division of
W.H. ALLEN & Co. PLC.

A Comet Book
Published in 1985
by the Paperback Division of
W.H. Allen & Co. PLC
44 Hill Street, London W1X 8LB

First published in the
United States of America by Sea-Wind Press
First British edition 1985

Copyright © Gail Pierce 1982

Printed in Great Britain by
Biddles Ltd, Guildford & King's Lynn

ISBN 0 86379 063 1

This book is sold subject to the condition that
it shall not, by way of trade or otherwise, be lent, re-sold
hired out or otherwise circulated without the publisher's
prior consent in any other form of binding or cover other
than that in which it is published and without a similar
condition including this condition being imposed upon
the subsequent purchaser.

Contents

Health Benefits
of Brown Rice

8 oz (225 g) cooked brown rice supplies the following:
3–5 per cent calcium
5–9 per cent iron
7–18 per cent thiamin
5–12 per cent niacin
5–15 per cent riboflavin

Rice is easy to digest, low in fat and sodium, which makes it
a great diet food, and relatively allergy free. We have been
led to believe that meat is a high protein food, when in
reality an egg is at the top of the net protein utilization
(NPU) chart. Brown rice is right behind with an NPU of
70, greater than that of beef which has an NPU of about
60. Brown rice has all the eight essential amino acids
needed to promote growth and maintain life. Brown
rice, however, is high in methionine and low in lysine,
making it a partially complete protein; while beans are
the opposite. A combination of these two foods will
therefore provide complete protein.

Brown rice contains an antibiotic resistance factor,
pacifarins, that increases people's natural resistance to
disease. Another natural substance that rice contains is
auxones, which helps produce vitamins and rejuvenate
cells in the body. High in B vitamins, brown rice stimulates
the kidneys so that toxins are eliminated and urination
is increased.

A diet of fruit and brown rice is said to relieve high

blood pressure, help in the treatment of people suffering from obesity, complications of diabetes, hypertension and cardiovascular disease. This diet was originated in the 1930s by internist Dr Walter Kempner, whose treatments were considered quite successful.

We can get our nourishment straight from the earth's abundant bounties, by-passing the need to kill animals.

For our
continuing survival
we should become aware
of life and living foods,
separating ourselves from
the killing and eating of
dead animals.

Gail Pierce
Carmel, Ca. 1982

4

Brown Rice Protein Combinations

Milk
or
Cheese \

Legumes /

Brown
Rice \

/ Wheat

\ Seeds

Milk or *cheese:* Parmesan cheese sprinkled on, or baked rice and cheese, or rice pudding.

Legumes: dried beans, peas and lentils, peanuts either sprinkled on top or in a dish, soy grits added to rice while cooking, or tamari.

Wheat: in rice muffins, breads and pancakes.

Seeds: sesame added while cooking or sprinkled on top.

5

Cooking Brown Rice

Brown rice is one of the most versatile foods we have and can be used in many forms from breakfast to pudding. The recipes in this book call for *short-grain* brown rice, which is more readily available than long-grain brown rice and has a sweeter flavour. Raw brown rice will keep fresh for six months at room temperature and indefinitely when kept in the freezer. Cooked rice will keep one week in the refrigerator, covered so that it will not absorb odours. You might want to cook large batches of rice for quick use during the week, which will keep for longer periods of time, if stored in the freezer in air-tight containers.

8 oz (225 g) rice
16 fl oz (450 ml water)
Cooking time: 50–60 minutes
Yield: At least 1 lb (450 g) of cooked rice

It's a good idea to wash the rice before cooking. Place rice in a sieve and rinse quickly under a tap. Adding rice to boiling water insures the shortest cooking time. Cook over a low heat with lid on until rice is tender.

For a quick meal you need to soak the rice in the morning or the night before. The rice is then drained and cooked for 20 minutes or less.

The means
by which
the Author has
sought to work out
his design, will, it is
hoped, be found to
combine entertainment
with utility, and
amusement with
practical information -
John Timbes - Hints for the Table
1869

KITCHEN THINGS

When there is plenty of
vegetables, no meat is necessary

A Lady,

The Cook's Complete Guide
1827

Breakfast

If you miss breakfast, your energy level will be low. The type of breakfast you eat determines how you will feel throughout the day. Food should keep us running smoothly, not just fill us up. By eating too little or too much of the wrong kind of food you can produce inefficiency.

Rice isn't really so strange at breakfast, its nutty flavour lends itself well to breakfast dishes, whether as a cereal by itself or else added to muffins, pancakes or waffles. The easiest and quickest use of left-over rice it to make a cereal. You can either steam the rice for a few minutes over boiling water in a steamer or spead it on a baking tray and warm it in the oven. Put about 6 oz (175 g) per person into bowls, add honey to taste, sprinkle with cinnamon, chopped nuts and maybe shredded coconut. Top with a dab of butter, milk or boiling water. For a change you might throw in a handful of raisins, or sliced bananas. This is one dish that constantly changes.

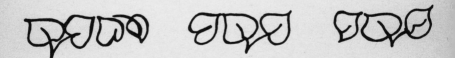

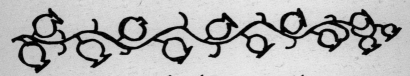

In southwest India, puttu, a
breakfast cereal is made from
soaked rice mixed with coconut,
freshly grated and cooked in
a bamboo steamer. This is
served with milk and sliced
bananas.

Breakfast Rice

Iron-rich raisins and something sweet! Serves 4.

8 oz (225 g) uncooked rice
32 fl oz (900 ml) milk
4 oz (125 g) raisins
natural maple syrup

   Grind the rice in blender until kernels are half the
original size. Combine rice with raisins and milk in a
saucepan. Bring to a boil, cover and simmer until rice is
cooked – about 15–20 minutes. Serve with natural
maple syrup.

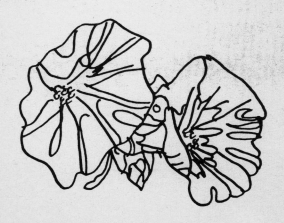

Cream of Brown Rice

Serves 4

8 oz (225 g) uncooked rice
32 fl oz (900 ml) water, or half water and half milk
pinch of salt

  Wash rice thoroughly, drain well and toast in dry pan until dry, about 5 minutes. In a nut mill or coffee mill, grind to a powder. Return rice powder to dry pan and toast lightly. Boil gently in lightly salted liquid for about 15 minutes.
  Sweeten with honey, molasses or natural maple syrup.

  Variations: cook with sliced apple, cinnamon or nutmeg; add chopped dates or raisins with rice powder.

Rice Sesame Cereal

8 oz (225 g) uncooked rice
2 Tbs. sesame seeds
16 fl oz (450 ml) water
1 tsp. salt
pinch of cinnamon
honey and milk to taste

Crack rice with sesame seeds in a blender for about 1 minute; stop before it turns into powder. Bring water, salt and cinnamon to a boil and add the ground rice and sesame mixture. Cover, reduce heat and simmer until the rice is tender – 20–25 minutes. Serve with honey and milk.

Pineapples have many health benefits...

Containing ananase, an enzyme, pineapples help to destroy many kinds of acute infections, and aid in reducing edematous swellings.

The chlorine content helps to remove wastes from the body by stimulating the kidneys.

Pineapples were discovered in Guadeloupe in 1493 by companions of Christopher Columbus. They found their way to Hawaii in 1790 and began to be cultivated there in the 1880's.

14

Pineapple Peanut *Rice*

Quick breakfast in a dish. Serves 4.

1 lb 8 oz (675 g) cooked rice
1 Tbs. butter
½ tsp. nutmeg
small tin of pineapple chunks, drained
4 oz (125 g) chopped peanuts

Heat the rice in the butter. Add all the other
ingredients and cook until hot. Serve immediately with
additional butter.

Dutch Apple Walnut Rice

Not only is this good for breakfast,
but it is equally nice for dessert.
Serves 4.

1 lb (450 g) cooked rice
5 fl oz (150 ml) milk
1 oz (25 g) raisins
1 oz (25 g) chopped walnuts
1 egg, beaten
2 Tbs. honey
½ tsp. salt
½ tsp. cinnamon
2 Tbs. butter
2–3 apples, peeled and sliced

Combine rice, raisins, eggs, honey, walnuts, salt,
cinnamon and half the butter in a saucepan. Place on
stove and simmer; stir occasionally until blended. Sauté
sliced apples in remaining butter until tender. Stir
apples into rice mixture. Serve warm for breakfast, or
try chilling for dessert.

Apples...

One of the many benefits of apples, raw or as juice, is that they are a valuable aid to digestion, especially eaten at the end of the meal.

Apples also cleanse the intestines, are a great blood purifier, they help to prevent tooth decay and because they are higher in phosphorus than any other fruit or vegetable, they are a great nerve and brain food, promoting a calm relaxing effect.

An apple eaten in the morning will help to overcome weakness in the body.

17

Rice Muffins

Quick and easy, moist and chewy. Prepare fruit and yoghurt while the muffins are baking. Makes 1 dozen.

6 oz (175 g) wholewheat flour
2 tsp. baking powder
1 tsp. salt
1 tsp cinnamon
1 Tbs. honey
2 Tbs. butter
8 oz (225 g) cold cooked rice
8 fl oz (225 ml) milk
1 egg, beaten

Preheat oven to 425°F (220°C), mark 7. Sift flour, baking powder, salt and cinnamon together in a large bowl. Cut in butter with a knife until mixture is crumbly. Add rice, milk, honey and egg. Mix until dry ingredients are moistened. Batter will be lumpy. Pour into oiled muffin tins. Bake for 25 minutes or until golden brown. Serve hot.

Antebellum Rice Bread

This recipe comes from the South and was served on the plantations as a breakfast dish.

1 Tbs. melted butter
1 Tbs. oil
8 oz (225 g) cooked rice
8 oz (225 g) cornmeal
½ tsp. salt
3 eggs, beaten

Preheat oven to 450°F (230°C), mark 8. Add rice to butter and oil in a saucepan, cover and heat over low heat. Mix cornmeal and salt in a bowl. Stir milk into beaten eggs and blend into the cornmeal. Blend together with the rice mixture and pour into a pan 8–9 in (20–22 cm) square. Bake for 25 minutes or until firm when tapped with finger and well browned on top.

Rice Pancakes

Rice adds a nutty flavour. Serves 4.

8 oz (225 g) cold cooked rice
3 eggs, separated
7 oz (200 g) flour, unbleached white or pastry wholewheat
2 tsp. baking powder
½ tsp. salt
½ tsp. cinnamon (optional)
pinch of nutmeg (optional)
1 Tbs. honey
14–16 fl oz (400–450 ml) milk, depending on thickness
    desired
2 Tbs. butter

Mix the flour, baking powder, salt, cinnamon and nutmeg. Stir in rice and egg yolks. Add honey and stir in milk. Beat egg whites until stiff and fold into the batter. Heat a pan and melt a small amount of the butter, drop 1 Tbs. of batter at a time into pan. Fry a few pancakes at a time, adding butter when needed. Serve with natural maple syrup, or honey and butter.

Buttermilk Rice pancakes

Serves 4

12 oz (350 g) cold cooked rice
16 fl oz (450 ml) buttermilk
2 tsp. baking powder
8 oz (225 g) flour
½ tsp. salt
½ tsp. cinnamon
1-2 eggs, beaten

Mix flour, baking powder, salt and cinnamon in a
mixing bowl. Stir in rice and eggs. Add buttermilk and
stir, mixing well. (When out of buttermilk, try yoghurt
beaten with a little milk.) Cook in hot pan, as for Rice
Pancakes.

Rice Waffles

Cinnamon and rice go together. Leave out the cinnamon and you have a base for creamed foods, served for lunch or dinner. Makes 6 waffles.

9 oz (250 g) wholewheat flour
1 Tbs. honey
2 tsp. baking powder
1 tsp. salt
1 tsp cinnamon
3 eggs, separated
20 fl oz (575 ml) milk
2 fl oz (50 ml) oil
8 oz (225 g) cold cooked rice

Sift dry ingredients together. Beat egg yolks, milk and oil together; combine with dry mixture. Stir in the rice. Beat the egg whites until stiff and fold into the batter. Cook on preheated waffle iron, serve with maple syrup, apple sauce, or your favourite topping.

Rice Buttermilk Southern Style Waffles

Serves 4

3 eggs, separated
16 fl oz (450 ml) buttermilk
3 Tbs. sifted unbleached flour
½ tsp. salt
1 tsp baking powder
1 tsp. honey
8 oz (225 g) cooked rice

Beat egg yolks until thick; add buttermilk and oil. Sift together dry ingredients; add to egg and buttermilk mixture. (A mixture of yoghurt and milk can be used as a substitute for buttermilk.) Stir in rice and honey. Beat egg whites until stiff and fold into rice mixture. Bake on a hot waffle iron.

Eggs

Eggs are an excellent source of protein, and are rich in nucleic acids.

The raw yolk is considered a great medicine for rebuilding depleted adrenal glands

Rice Omelette

This is an impressive omelette. Add bean sprouts and a splash of tamari for an oriental touch. Serve for lunch or dinner. Serves 1-2.

1 Tbs. wholewheat flour
4 fl oz (125 ml) milk
3 eggs separated
½ tsp. salt
8 oz (225 g) cooked rice

Mix flour in a small saucepan with a small amount of the milk until smooth. Stir in remaining milk. Bring to a boil, stirring. Beat the egg yolks, mix with salt and rice and add to milk mixture. Beat egg whites until stiff and fold into rice mixture. Pour mixture into a very hot, buttered omelette pan. Cook until well browned on bottom. Place under preheated grill to brown. Fold over on to plate and serve.

Plantation Rice

Fruit, grain and eggs all in one dish. For brunch you might also serve muffins. Serves 4.

2 Tbs. oil
1 medium onion, chopped
1 lb 8 oz (675 g) cooked rice
1–2 Tbs. tamari
4 eggs
¼ tsp. ginger powder (optional)
4 bananas, cut in half lengthwise.

Heat a medium pan with half the oil; sauté onions for 5 minutes. Add tamari, ginger and rice and fry together. Heat another pan; add remaining oil and fry the eggs. Remove eggs and keep warm in an oven that has been preheated to 250°F (130°C), mark ½, for a few minutes and turned off. Fry bananas in pan that eggs were cooked in, browning slightly. Place one serving of the rice on a round dish. Make an indentation in the centre of the rice. Fill with one egg, arrange 2 slices of banana around the egg, serve garnished with parsley.

Eggs in a Nest

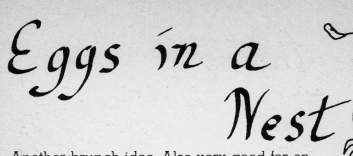

Another brunch idea. Also very good for an early Sunday dinner with steamed asparagus Serves 4.

1 lb (450 g) reheated cooked rice
1 Tbs. butter
1 Tbs. wholewheat flour
1 tsp. salt
½-1 tsp. curry powder
pinch of paprika
8 fl oz (225 ml) hot milk
4 oz (125 g) Cheddar cheese, grated
4 eggs, poached

Reheat rice by spreading on a baking tray in an oven, 325°F (170°C), mark 3, for at least 10 minutes, stirring occasionally to prevent sticking. Melt butter in saucepan; add and stir in flour along with seasonings. Add milk, stirring constantly until mixture thickens. Add cheese and stir until cheese is melted. Cover and remove from heat, stirring occasionally to prevent crust forming. Poach eggs. Place a serving of rice on each plate. Make an identation in the centre of the rice. Place a poached egg in each one. Pour the cheese sauce over each plate, distributing evenly, and serve.

Hashed Brown Rice

The alternative to hashed brown potatoes. Serves 4.

1 lb 8 oz (675 g) cooked rice
1 Tbs. wholewheat flour
2 fl oz (50 ml) milk
1 Tbs. butter
1 Tbs. oil
1 small onion, chopped
½ tsp. salt
pepper to taste

Combine rice, flour and milk. Set aside. Sauté onion in butter and oil until tender in a large pan. Mix with rice mixture; add salt and pepper. Spread rice mixture in a greased pan. Press down firmly. Cook over medium heat, browning the bottom. Turn on to dish and serve.

Man is the
butcher and
the tomb of
his brother animals,
        Alexander Pope,
            Times of Innocence
                1733

Rice Salads

Rice turned into salads can be the highlight of a quick meal. I like them for lunch with crackers. For a quick salad use cooked cold rice with chopped vegetables. Onion, celery, green pepper and chopped carrots are good. Blend with a dressing of mayonnaise and seasoning salt. For a change add a chopped egg.

Lemon Rice Salad

Serves 4

1 lb (450 g) cooked rice
1 Tbs. olive oil
1 Tbs. chopped chives
1 Tbs. chopped parsley
juice of 1 lemon
salt to taste

Combine all the ingredients. Toss and chill. Especially good with summer foods.

Rice and Almond salad

This is an easy rice salad with a great taste. Good with a fruit salad for lunch. Serves 4-6.

1 lb (450 g) cooked chilled rice
½ tsp. salt
¼ tsp. curry powder, or to taste
4 oz (125 g) mayonnaise
2 sticks of celery, chopped fine
juice of ½ lemon
2 oz (50 g) toasted almonds, slivered

Place the chilled rice in a bowl and toss with the rest of the ingredients. Serve immediately.

32

Curry Rice Salad

A taste of India. For a light summer dinner serve a citrus fruit salad and popovers. Serves 4–6.

2 oz (50 g) raisins
8 fl oz (225 ml) warm water
1 lb 8 oz (675 g) cooked rice
1 tsp. curry powder
2 oz (50 g) chopped almonds
4 oz (125 g) tiny peas, cooked
8 oz (225 g) mayonnaise
juice of ½ lemon
salt to taste

   Soak raisins for 1 hour in warm water. Combine rice, drained raisins, almonds and peas in a bowl. Flavour mayonnaise with lemon juice and curry powder. Mix salad with mayonnaise mixture and season with salt to taste.

Green peas - are an excellent source of vitamin 'A' and a good source of vitamin 'C', riboflavin, phosphorous, iron, potassium, niacin and calcium - They also have a small amount of protein -

Best Home-Made Mayonnaise

For use in the salads in this section—

1 egg
½ tsp. dry mustard
¼ tsp. salt
2 Tbs. vinegar or lemon juice
8 fl oz (225 ml) safflower or sunflower oil

Put the egg, mustard, salt and vinegar and half the oil in a blender. Blend until smooth. Continue blending while adding remaining oil in a steady stream into the centre of the egg mixture until all is mixed. Store covered in the refrigerator.

Italian Rice Salad

Lots of oil and vinegar and crisp vegetables makes this tangy salad a hit any time. Serves 4.

1 lb 8 oz (675 g) hot cooked rice
½ tsp. salt
2 Tbs. olive oil
1 Tbs. wine vinegar
pepper to taste
3 sticks of celery, chopped diagonally
1 small onion, chopped
2 oz (50 g) olives, chopped
tomatoes, cut in wedges

Salad dressing
3 Tbs. olive oil
1 Tbs. wine vinegar
½ tsp. salt

   Mix oil, vinegar, salt and pepper. Pour over hot rice. Mix well and cool. Set aside chopped vegetables. Mix together rice, vegetables (except tomatoes) and salad dressing. Place in refrigerator for two hours or more. Stir occasionally. Garnish with tomatoes and serve.

Hot Italian Rice Salad

A one-dish meal. Serve with thick slices of French bread
Serves 4.

1 lb 8 oz (675 g) hot cooked rice
3 sticks of celery, chopped
1 small green pepper, chopped
2 Tbs. parsley, chopped
4 oz (125 g) hot tiny peas
2 oz (50 g) black olives, sliced
2 oz (50 g) Parmesan cheese, grated
4 fl oz (125 ml) olive oil
juice of 1 lemon
salt to taste

   Mix together hot rice, celery, green pepper, parsley,
peas, olives and cheese. Toss with olive oil, then lemon
juice. Add a little salt if necessary and serve.

Olives and Olive Oil are
extremely high in Vitamin 'C'
and are one of the best sources
of potassium, plus being
beneficial as a brain and
nerve food.

Picnic Rice Salad

This salad is terrific for picnics as it doesn't use mayonnaise for the dressing. Made the day before, the flavours will improve. Serves 6–8.

1 lb 12 oz (800 g) cooked rice
2 green peppers, chopped
1 small onion, chopped or 1 small bunch of spring onions, chopped
2 oz (50 g) walnuts or almonds, coarsely chopped
1 Tbs. parsley, chopped

Salad dressing
3 fl oz (75 ml) olive oil
1 Tbs. wine vinegar
½ tsp. dry mustard
1 tsp. paprika
¼ tsp. salt
pepper to taste

Garnish
2 tomatoes
2 hard-boiled eggs
1 Tbs. parsley

Combine ingredients in a large salad bowl. Combine dressing ingredients in a jar, shake and pour over rice mixture. Toss all ingredients until well mixed. Refrigerate. Just before serving, arrange lettuce on a platter. Mound the rice mixture in the centre, surround with tomato wedges and quartered hard-boiled eggs. Sprinkle chopped parsley over top.

37

Luncheon Rice Salad

Serves 6

1 lb 8 oz (675 g) cold cooked rice
small bunch spring onions, minced fine
3 sticks of celery, chopped fine
1 medium cucumber, peeled and sliced
2 oz (50 g) olives, chopped
1 dozen small tomatoes, halved
½ tsp. salt
1 hard-boiled egg yolk
16 fl oz (450 ml) mayonnaise
4 fl oz (125 ml) sour cream — or plain yoghurt
juice of 1 lemon

   Mix everything except the last 3 ingredients in a
salad bowl. Mash the egg yolk very smooth; combine
with mayonnaise, sour cream and lemon juice. Toss
with rice combination until all ingredients are coated.

Greek Hot Rice Salad

Serve with baked beans and
a spinach salad. Serves 4

1 lb (450 g) hot cooked rice
½ tsp. salt
pepper to taste
1 small onion, chopped
2 fl oz (50 ml) olive oil
1 Tbs. lemon juice, or to taste
oregano
parsley or black olives

While rice is still hot, add the salt, pepper and
chopped onion. Blend the oil and lemon juice and pour
over the rice. Sprinkle with oregano and toss. Garnish
with parsley or olives.

Oregano......
Mexicans use it
as an antiseptic for cuts
and wounds. It is also
good as an antispasmodic,
expectorant and tonic.
As an aid for headaches,
nerves, upset stomachs and
indigestion.

Curried Pineapple Rice Salad

A light summer meal with rolls. Serves 4.

1 lb (450 g) cold cooked rice
2 sticks of celery, chopped
½ small green pepper, chopped
1 Tbs. onion, minced
1–2 tsp. curry powder
½ tsp. dry mustard
½ tsp. salt
4 fl oz (125 ml) mayonnaise
1 Tbs. lemon juice
1 small tin of crushed pineapple, drained
1 oz (25 g) chopped peanuts

Mix together rice, celery and green pepper. Mix onion, curry powder, mustard, and salt with mayonnaise. Stir in lemon juice. Toss rice mixture with mayonnaise mixture. Add pineapple and chopped peanuts; mix again and serve.

Know on Thyself thy
genius must depend—
All books of cookery,
all helps of art, all
critic learning, all
commenting notes,
are vain, if void of
genius thou wouldest
cook—
Dionysius The
α Carthussian
1450

Men dig their
Graves with their
own Teeth and
die more by those
fatal instruments
than the weapons
of their enemies—
Thomas Moffett — 1600
Helth's Improvement

Soups

There is nothing like soup on a cold winter day, or a cool summer evening. Soup and sandwiches are always welcome for lunch or dinner.

Soup is one of the almost perfect dishes, because the vegetable nutrients are not lost in the cooking water, but remain in the broth to flavour it and to nourish us. That is why it has been said that a person can live on soup and bread alone.

By soup, I mean the home-made variety, where the freshest possible vegetables are used and where the ingredients used are there for nourishment, not for preserving our insides. No unnecessary fillers, no monosodium glutamate, no preservatives or additives — and no added sugar.

My favourite day for making soup is also bread-making day.

To make vegetable broth, save a bag of vegetable trimmings: carrot tops with the green still attached; celery leaves; pea pods; courgette peelings; parsley stems; tips of green beans, etc. The trimmings should be clean and used when you have 1 lb (450 g) or more. Place in a pan; add salt, which brings out the vegetable flavours; cover with water and bring to a boil. Cover with lid and simmer for 30 minutes. Strain the stock, cool and refrigerate in a glass jar or use immediately as a soup base.

Basic Vegetable Rice Soup

The soup I make on bread-baking day is a vegetable soup with any amount of left-over rice. Uncooked rice can be added at beginning of cooking time instead. Serves 4.

I like to cook soup in a cast-iron pot as some of the iron will seep into the soup.

courgettes
turnips
celery
carrots
mushrooms
cabbage
green beans
onions
1 Tbs. oil

1 Tbs. butter
pinch of basil
1 bay leaf
1 clove of garlic, minced
red wine (optional)
1 lb (450 g) tomatoes, fresh
   or tinned
left-over rice
salt to taste

Slice or shred vegetables. Sauté onion in mixture of oil and butter with basil, bay leaf and garlic added to it. Add celery, carrots, mushrooms, courgettes, turnips, and sauté. Add a good splash or red wine for added flavour if desired. Then add shredded cabbage, tomatoes, salt and water to cover. Bring to boil, cover and simmer for about 30 minutes. Add cooked rice for last 10 minutes or so of cooking and serve.

Lemon Rice Soup

This is a Malaysian-style soup, great for a light lunch or
with a spinach and mushroom salad for dinner.
Serves 4.

48 fl oz (1.3 l) vegetable stock or water
6 oz (150 g) uncooked rice
1 bay leaf
1 tsp. salt
¼ tsp. summer savory
3 eggs, beaten
juice and grated peel of 1 lemon
parsley or chives, chopped

Bring stock to a boil in a saucepan; add rice, bay leaf
and salt. Simmer for 30 minutes or until rice is tender.
Remove bay leaf. Mix summer savory with beaten eggs,
add lemon juice and peel. Stirring constantly, slowly
add 8 fl oz (225 ml) of stock to egg mixture. Add egg
mixture to soup; heat through and garnish each bowl
before serving with parsley or chives.

Lemons are thought to be a
native of southeast Asia,
possibly Malaysia. They were
once used only for medicinal
purposes. They are an
excellent source of bioflavinoids
calcium, phosphorus, 'A' and 'C'.

Spinach and Rice Soup

This soup has more flavour when made with vegetable stock. Serves 4.

1 small onion, chopped
1 Tbs. butter
35 fl oz (1 l) vegetable stock or water
6 oz (175 g) uncooked rice
1 packet chopped frozen spinach, thawed, or 8 oz (225 g)
  fresh chopped spinach
1 tsp. salt
nutmeg to taste

Sauté onion in butter in a large saucepan until golden. Add stock and bring to a boil. Put rice in and simmer uncovered for 40 minutes or until rice is almost done. Add spinach, salt and nutmeg. Simmer 10–15 minutes or until rice is tender.

Not only does Spinach contain the finest quality of organic iron available but is rich in sodium, potassium, calcium and magnesium - the cells, tissues, muscles, and nerves can benefit from this food -

Brown Rice Soup

Serves 4

1 medium onion, sliced
3 medium-sized carrots, sliced
4 oz (125 g) green beans, sliced
2 Tbs. oil
½ tsp. salt
1–2 Tbs. tamari
8 oz (225 g) cooked rice
4 oz (125 g) cooked haricot beans
35 fl oz (1 l) water

Sauté onion, carrots and green beans in oil in a saucepan. Sauté vegetables until onion is tender. Add water and salt and bring to a boil; then lower flame. Add cooked rice and haricot beans and simmer until vegetables are tender, 20–30 minutes. Add tamari before serving.

Green beans are a good source of vitamins 'A', 'C', and 'B'. Because of their high potassium content green beans are used to help restore the pancreas and liver and for an aid in neutralizing diets-

Tomatoes · are an excellent
source of vitamins 'A' and 'C' -
they also contain calcium,
phosphorus, potassium, and
sodium -

Tomatoes are both a
fruit and vegetable and are
probably a native of Northwestern
South America. Before Columbus
discovered America tomatoes
found their way to Mexico
where they were domesticated -

Cream of Tomato Rice Soup

Serves 4

1 small onion, chopped
2 Tbs. butter
35 fl oz (1 l) tomato juice
6 oz (175 g) cooked rice
4 fl oz (125 ml) cream
pinch of basil
1 tsp. salt

Sauté onion in butter in a large saucepan. Add tomato juice, rice, cream and seasonings and heat to simmering point. Do not boil or it will curdle.

For a more tangy soup, yoghurt can be substituted for the cream.

Tomato Rice Soup

This is my family's favourite soup.
Serves 4

1 large tin of tomatoes
1 medium onion, chopped
2 sticks of celery, chopped
1 carrot, grated
1 Tbs. oil or butter
pinch of basil
1 clove of garlic, minced
1 bay leaf
24 fl oz (675 ml) water
1 tsp. salt
4 fl oz (125 ml) red wine (optional)
6 oz (175 g) uncooked rice
Parmesan cheese, grated

Heat oil in a saucepan. Sauté vegetables until onion is tender. Blend tomatoes in blender; add to pan with basil, garlic, bay leaf, salt, water, wine and rice. Bring to a boil, cover, lower heat and cook 30 minutes or until rice is tender. Serve and sprinkle with Parmesan cheese.

Puree of Rice Soup

Serves 4

2 Tbs. butter
1 large onion, chopped
1 large carrot, scraped and sliced thin
4 oz (125 g) rice
35 fl oz (1 l) water
1 bay leaf
1 tsp. curry powder (optional)
1 tsp. salt
8 fl oz (225 ml) cream or milk, warmed
parsley, chopped

Heat butter in a saucepan and cook onion and carrot until onion is tender. Add rice, water, bay leaf, curry powder (if desired) and salt. Bring to a boil; reduce heat and simmer the rice, covered, for about 40 minutes or until rice is tender. Remove bay leaf, place in a blender until smooth. Add the rice mixture to the warmed cream, stirring to blend the soup well. Garnish with a sprinkling of parsley.

Rice and Potato Soup

A different kind of
potato soup. Serves 4.

4 medium potatoes, peeled and diced
2 onions, sliced
2 sticks of celery, chopped
1 Tbs. butter
1 tsp. salt
pepper to taste
1 clove of garlic, minced
28 fl oz (800 ml) vegetable stock
10 fl oz (275 ml) milk
4 oz (125 g) cooked rice

Sauté onion and celery in butter with garlic. Add the potatoes, stock, salt and pepper. Cook over low heat until the vegetables are soft, about 20 minutes. Blend a little at a time in blender; return to pot. Add milk and rice, heat through and serve.

Potatoes - are a superior quality of protein and an excellent source of vitamins 'A' and 'B'. Because the potato has an abundance of alkalis, compounds of soda and potash it is a great aid in neutralizing the acid wastes in the body -

Chickpea and Rice soup

Chick peas can be bought in a tin – with a few
additives – or you can prepare your own. Serves 5.

8 oz (225 g) cold cooked rice
1 lb (450 g) cooked chick peas
2 Tbs. butter
1 medium onion, chopped
1 clove of garlic, minced
64 fl oz (1.8 l) vegetable stock or water
1 tomato, chopped
pinch of cumin
½ tsp. salt
1 Tbs. tamari
1 lemon, cut into wedges

   Melt butter in a saucepan, sauté onion and garlic
until tender. Add water, rice, chick peas, tomato, cumin
and salt. Cook over a low heat for 40 minutes. Purée
the soup, half the rice and chick peas in a blender.
Heat again with tamari. Serve with a wedge of lemon in
each bowl.

Cream of Mushroom Rice soup

A very rich high-protein soup.
Serves 4–6.

1 large onion, chopped
2 Tbs. butter
1 lb (450 g) mushrooms, sliced
48 fl oz (1.3 l) water
1 Tbs. tamari
4 oz (125 g) uncooked rice
1 tsp. salt
8 fl oz (225 m) yoghurt
2 Tbs. parsley, chopped

Sauté the onions in the butter in a saucepan. Add
and sauté mushrooms until tender. Add water and
tamari along with rice, bring to a boil, lower heat, cover
and simmer 30 minutes or until rice is tender. Add salt.
In a blender, purée the onions, half of the mushrooms
and rice along with some of the liquid. Return to the
pan. Mix the yoghurt with a little of the soup. Barely
heat, making sure not to curdle mixture. Sprinkle
parsley over each serving.

Lentil Rice Soup

Serves 4

8 oz (225 g) lentils
48 fl oz (1.3 l) water
2 tsp. salt
pinch of cumin
6 oz (175 g) rice
1 medium onion, chopped
2 Tbs. butter
1 Tbs. tamari or to taste

Rinse lentils and place in a saucepan with water, salt, cumin and rice. (Lentils can be interchanged with split peas or used half and half.) Bring to a boil, lower heat and cover. Cook for about 45 minutes or until tender. Sauté onion in butter and stir into soup along with tamari just before serving.

Lentils - brown, red, and green are a nutritious source of iron, cellulose and 'B' vitamins.

Split peas - both green and yellow are a good source of protein and minerals -

Rice Lentil Soya Bean Soup

This high-protein soup is quick to make – about 20
minutes from pot to table. A good reason to have
cooked soya beans and rice on hand. Serves 6.

4 oz (125 g) washed lentils
32 fl oz (900 ml) vegetable stock or water
4 oz (125 g) cooked rice
1 tsp. salt
1 large onion, chopped
1 clove of garlic, minced
1 Tbs. oil
8 oz (225 g) cooked soya beans
1 small tin of tomatoes, chopped
Parmesan cheese, grated

Blend lentils and a quarter of the stock in blender
until lentils are pulverized. Pour into saucepan; add
remaining stock, rice and salt. Bring to a boil, lower to
simmer. Sauté onion and garlic in oil for about 5
minutes. Add to rice and lentil mixture. Add soya beans
and tomato sauce to the pot; stir well. Heat through and
serve. Sprinkle Parmesan over each serving.

Minestrone Soup

A perfectly combined soup that can be served as a meal for guests. Serves 6.

1 Tbs. butter
1 Tbs. oil
1 onion, chopped
1 clove of garlic, minced
8 oz (225 g) kidney beans, cooked
4 oz (125 g) peas
8 oz (225 g) green cabbage, shredded
2 sticks of celery, chopped
8 oz (225 g) spinach, shredded, or 1 packet frozen spinach
3 carrots, washed and sliced
2 medium tomatoes, peeled and chopped
1 large potato, peeled and cubed
1 courgette, sliced
32 fl oz (900 ml) vegetable stock or water
pinch of dried sage
pinch of basil
1 bay leaf
4 fl oz (125 ml) red wine (optional)
6 oz (175 g) uncooked rice
Parmesan cheese, grated

Heat the butter and oil in a saucepan; sauté garlic and onion with sage, basil and bay leaf. Add the rest of the vegetables except the spinach. Sauté for about 10 minutes. Add stock, wine, if desired, beans, and salt. Simmer for 1 hour. Add rice and cook for another 30 minutes, until rice is tender. Add spinach and heat through. Serve with grated Parmesan.

57

Animals do not sit
down to a table loaded
with a variety of dishes
collected from every zone.

They eat of one kind at
a time and therefore never
over-eat.

They have grass and water
today, and grass and water
tomorrow, and so on through
their entire lives,
            and yet they
        are in perfect health

Dr. A.F. Reinhold
Nature Versus Drugs -
                1898

Lunch and Supper Dishes

The recipes that follow are for dishes that can be served at either lunch or dinner. I serve brown rice often during the week. We never tire of it because of the many ways it can be prepared.

Rice Parmigiana

Serves 3-4

1 lb (450 g) cooked rice
3 Tbs. chopped fresh or 1 Tbs. dried parsley
2 Tbs. of spring onions or ordinary onion, finely chopped
4 oz (125 g) Parmesan cheese, grated
2 eggs, beaten
2 fl oz (50 ml) milk
1 tsp. salt

Toss rice with parsley, spring onions and cheese. Beat eggs and milk and add salt. Combine the two mixtures and pour into a well-buttered casserole dish. Place dish in a pan of hot water and bake at 350°F (180°C), mark 4, for 30-40 minutes or until firm.

Sesame Rice

For when you need rice as an accompaniment to a meal. Serves 6.

1 lb (450 g) uncooked rice
2 Tbs. roasted sesame seeds
32 fl oz (900 ml) boiling water
1 tsp. salt or
1 Tbs. tamari
1 tsp. butter

Boil water, add rice, sesame seeds, salt or tamari, and butter. Reduce heat, cover and simmer for 50–60 minutes.

Baked Rice With Almonds

Serves 4

1 lb (450 g) cooked rice
2 eggs, beaten
12 fl oz (350 ml) milk
1 Tbs. butter
2 Tbs. tamari
2 oz (50 g) chopped almonds

Mix all ingredients. Pour into a casserole dish. Bake
20–30 minutes at 350°F (180°C), mark 4, or until set
and lightly browned. To enhance the almond flavour,
let the mixture sit an hour before baking.

Red Rice

A simple recipe to be served as a side dish. Marvellous colour with a green vegetable meal. Serves 4.

1 Tbs. butter
8 oz (225 g) rice
1 tsp. salt
8 fl oz (225 ml) water
2 tsp. paprika
pinch of cayenne pepper

Melt butter in a saucepan, add rice, stir adding salt, paprika and cayenne pepper. Do not brown. Add water, bring to a boil, cover and reduce heat. Simmer for 50-60 minutes.

Cider Rice Pilaf

Tangy accompaniment to a meal. Serves 4.

3 Tbs. butter
8 oz (225 g) rice
1 tsp. salt
1 small onion, chopped
2 sticks of celery, chopped
2 Tbs. parsley, chopped
20 fl oz (575 ml) apple cider, natural, unsweetened

Melt butter in pan over low heat. Add rice, stirring until golden. Add salt, onion and celery; continue sautéeing until vegetables are tender. Add parsley. Bring cider to a boil in a medium saucepan. Stir in rice, cover and cook over low heat for about 50 minutes or until liquid is absorbed and rice is tender.

Lemon Yoghurt
rice

Vitamin C with rice. Serves 4.

8 oz (225 g) rice
16 fl oz (450 ml) water
grated peel of ½ lemon
juice of ½ lemon
4 fl oz (125 ml) plain yoghurt
1 Tbs. parsley, chopped

Bring water, lemon peel and juice to a boil. Add rice.
Cover and cook over low heat for 50 minutes or until
done. Add yoghurt and parsley; stir to heat through
over low heat and serve.

This idea comes from China
Rice that is stuck to the
bottom of a pan is scraped
out in chunks. When dried
it is deep fried, making
it puff up and become
crunchy.
        The puffs can be
eaten with a little salt —

Cashew Sesame Rice

This is a good dish to serve with vegetable enchiladas. Serves 4.

2 Tbs. oil
2 Tbs. cashews, roughly chopped
4 oz (125 g) sesame seeds
2 lb (900 g) hot cooked rice
salt to taste
1/4 tsp. cayenne pepper or 1 tsp. chilli powder

Heat oil in pan. Sauté cashews until they begin to brown. Add seeds and seasoning choice, frying until seeds are golden. Stir into rice, add salt if needed and serve.

If you're out of cashews, try almonds. Omit cayenne pepper and season with tamari for an oriental side dish or as a base for stir-fried vegetables.

Oriental Celery rice

This rice has a superb sauce coating. Serves 4.

5 large sticks of celery, cut in ½ in pieces
1 medium onion, chopped
2 Tbs. oil or butter
1 Tbs. wholewheat flour
1 tsp. salt or to taste
16 fl oz (450 ml) water
2 Tbs. tamari or more
8 oz (225 g) uncooked rice

Heat oil in medium saucepan and sauté onion until golden. Stir in flour and salt. Turn up the heat and add the water with the tamari, still stirring. Continue to stir until sauce comes to a boil. Add the celery and rice. Mix well. Cover and reduce heat to low. Cook for about 50 minutes or until rice is done and celery is tender.

Not only is celery economic but is excellent for nervous disorders, skin problems. Rich in potassium, magnesium and iron—

Nourishing rice

Serves 4

8 oz (225 g) uncooked rice
24 fl oz (675 ml) boiling water
1 medium onion, chopped
1 clove garlic, minced (optional)
2 Tbs. butter
1 tsp. salt
20 fl oz (575 ml) hot milk
3 Tbs. parsley, chopped

Boil the rice in water for 12 minutes. Drain. In a deep heavy saucepan, sauté onion and garlic in butter. Stir in the rice and salt. Pour in the milk slowly and stir thoroughly. Reduce heat as low as possible, cover and cook for 45 minutes or until the liquid is absorbed. Fluff with a fork, sprinkle with parsley and serve.

Parsley - is a very beneficial herb, a good source of vitamins A and B and rich in iron, calcium, potassium and sulphur. Parsley is a good blood builder, and it will help to eliminate breath odors.

Nuts and Rice

If you like nuts, mushrooms and sour cream, you'll love this high-protein dish. Serves 4.

1 lb (450 g) hot cooked rice
2 oz (50 g) sliced brazil nuts
1 Tbs. pumpkin seeds, toasted
½ tsp. salt
4 oz (225 g) sliced mushrooms, sautéed in 1 Tbs. butter
4 fl oz (125 ml) sour cream

Combine all the ingredients in a casserole and heat in oven, 350°F (180°C), mark 4, for about 15 minutes and serve.

Green Green Green Rice

I love this dish served with sliced tomatoes and steamed vegetables. Serves 4.

2 Tbs. oil
8 oz (225 g) uncooked rice
16 fl oz (450 ml) water
1 Tbs. sesame seeds
1 Tbs. celery leaves, chopped
½ green pepper, chopped
4 Tbs. parsley, chopped
4 Tbs. chives, chopped
½ onion, chopped

Heat oil in saucepan. Sauté onion and green pepper for a few minutes. Add everything except the water and stir to distribute ingredients. Pour in water, bring to a boil, reduce heat, cover, simmer for 50–60 minutes.

Baked Green Rice Casserole

Serves 4

2 eggs, beaten
8 fl oz (225 ml) milk
4 Tbs. parsley, chopped
1 clove garlic, minced (optional)
1 small onion, chopped
1 lb (900 g) cooked rice
3 oz (75 g) Cheddar cheese, grated
1 tsp. curry powder

Either sauté the onion and garlic in a little butter and mix with the other ingredients, or just mix all the ingredients, bake in an oiled casserole in oven, 325°F (170°C), mark 3, for 30–40 minutes.

For more texture and colour, serve with a salad loaded with tomatoes and shredded carrots.

Green Rice

Serves 4

1 Tbs. oil
1 medium onion, chopped
2 small green chillis, diced, with seeds removed
1 stick of celery with leaves, chopped
4 Tbs. parsley, finely chopped
4 oz (225 g) broccoli, chopped fine
4 oz (225 g) fresh spinach, chopped fine
1 tsp. salt
24 fl oz (675 ml) water
1 lb (900 g) rice
Parmesan cheese, grated

Sauté onion until tender in oil over medium heat in a large pan. Add rest of the vegetables, salt and water; bring to a boil. Add butter and rice, cover, lower heat and cook until rice is done, about 50 minutes. Serve with grated Parmesan cheese.

Greek Spinach and Rice

A light summer dish to serve with home-baked bread.
Serves 4.

4 fl oz (125 ml) olive oil
1 medium onion, chopped
2 tomatoes, sliced
1 lb (900 g) fresh spinach, chopped, or 1 packet frozen,
    thawed and drained
1 lb 8 oz (675 g) cooked rice
1 tsp. chopped fresh mint or ½ tsp. dried mint
1 tsp. salt

Sauté onion in oil until soft; add tomatoes and simmer
until thickened slightly. Add spinach, rice, mint and
salt, with water as needed. Cover and simmer for about
10 minutes to heat through and blend flavours. Serve.

Ricotta Rice

This marvellously rich dish can be frozen before cooking or refrigerated all day if made in the morning. Just bring to room temperature before baking. Serves 4.

1 lb 8 oz (675 g) cooked rice
4 Tbs. chives, chopped
12 oz (350 g) ricotta cheese or creamed cottage cheese
1 clove of garlic, minced (optional)
8 fl oz (225 ml) sour cream
1 Tbs. milk
dash of hot chilli sauce
1 tsp. salt
Parmesan cheese, grated

Combine rice and onions. Blend ricotta, garlic, if desired, sour cream, milk, hot chilli sauce and salt. Stir into rice and onions. Turn into buttered casserole dish, sprinkle with Parmesan cheese and bake at 350°F (180°C), mark 4, for about 30 minutes.

Garlic Rosemary Rice

Garlic, rosemary and
lemon are a good combination.
Serves 5-6.

2-3 cloves of garlic, minced
1 tsp. salt
1 Tbs. butter
1 Tbs. oil
12 oz (350 g) rice
peel of 1 lemon, grated
juice of half a lemon
1 tsp. dried rosemary
24 fl oz (675 ml) water

Crush garlic and salt to a smooth paste. Heat oil and
butter in a medium saucepan. Add garlic and salt and
stir for about 1 minute. Add rice, stirring for about 3
minutes. Add lemon peel, juice, rosemary and water,
bring to a boil and cover; lower to simmer and cook for
about 50 minutes or until tender.

Garlic -
is an antispamodic, diuretic
and expectorant. Its antiseptic
substances tone up the digestive
system, and is also known to
reduce blood pressure -

Celery Tomato Rice

A tasty dish that will spice up any meal. Serves 4.

24 fl oz (675 ml) tomato juice
8 oz (225 g) rice
1 tsp. salt
2 peppercorns
2 whole cloves
1 bay leaf
2 sticks of celery, chopped
1 small onion, chopped
1 Tbs. oil

Heat oil in medium saucepan, sauté celery and onion. Add tomato juice and bring to a boil. Add rice, salt, peppercorns, cloves and bay leaf. Bring back to a boil and lower heat to simmer. Cook covered for about 1¼ hours, or until rice is tender but still chewy. Remove the bay leaf before serving.

Cloves are a good antiseptic, the oil is used for toothaches and teething babies if dropped in cavity or rubbed on gums—

Simple Rice Pilaf

The difference between plain rice and rice pilaf is that the rice for a pilaf is sautéed in butter or oil, then cooked in stock or water. Serves 4.

8 oz (225 g) rice
1 Tbs. butter
1 small onion, chopped
16 fl oz (450 ml) vegetable stock or water
1 tsp. salt

Sauté onion in butter until soft. Lower heat and add rice slowly, stirring until rice is almost transparent. Add stock or water and salt. Bring to a boil, lower heat and simmer, covered, for about 50 minutes, or until rice is done. If using water, you might like to add 1 tsp. curry powder for added flavour. I also sometimes sauté a stick of celery and some sliced mushrooms with the onion.

Tomato Pilaf

Simply red rice. Serves 4.

8 oz (225 g) rice
1 medium onion, chopped
1 large tin of tomatoes, chopped
16 fl oz (450 ml) water
1 tsp. salt
1 Tbs. oil
1 Tbs. butter

   Heat oil and butter in medium pan; sauté onion.
Reduce heat and add rice slowly, stirring until almost
transparent. Add all other ingredients and cook as for
simple pilaf.

Rice With Sweet and Sour Lentils

A grand topping for rice.
Serves 4.

4 oz (225 g) lentils, washed and cooked
1 lb 8 oz (675 g) hot cooked rice
1 Tbs. oil
1 Tbs. honey
2 Tbs. cider vinegar
½ tsp. salt
1 Tbs. onion, minced
pinch of cayenne
pinch of ground cloves
2 tsp. lemon juice
1 tsp. grated fresh ginger or ¼ tsp. dried ginger
1 large apple, cut in chunks
1 tsp arrowroot powder
1 Tbs. water

In frying pan combine oil, honey, vinegar, onion, seasonings, lemon juice and grated ginger. Heat, stirring often, for about 5 minutes. Dissolve arrowroot in water. Add to hot mixture, stirring constantly; the sauce will thicken a little. Drain and rinse cooked lentils, then add them to the sauce. Cook to heat. Stir in the raw apple, cooking just long enough to heat through. Serve over hot rice.

Italian Rice with Lentils

Rice and lentils are a great
protein combination.
Serves 4.

48 fl oz (1.3 l) water
½ tsp. salt
4 oz (225 g) lentils, washed
1–2 Tbs. olive oil
1 clove of garlic, chopped in quarters
1 small onion, chopped
1 small tin of tomatoes, chopped
1 tsp. salt
½ tsp. basil
1 lb 8 oz (675 g) hot cooked rice

Bring salted water to a boil in a large pot. Add lentils
and simmer for 1 hour or until tender. Drain and rinse.
Just before lentils are cooked, heat olive oil in a large
saucepan. Sauté garlic until limp but not brown.
Remove garlic pieces and sauté onion. Add tomatoes,
basil and salt to onion; simmer for 10 minutes. Add
drained lentils and rice, cook over low heat for 10
minutes, stirring often, and serve.

Rice Patties

Serve as burgers with everything, or as an entrée with tomato sauce. Serves 4.

12 oz (350 g) cooked rice
4 oz (225 g) peanuts, finely chopped or ground
2 oz (125 g) sunflower seeds, finely chopped or ground
1 small onion, chopped
2 eggs, beaten
¼ tsp. thyme
½ tsp sage
1 tsp. salt
1 Tbs. oil

Mix together all ingredients except oil. In a large heavy-bottomed pan, heat the oil over moderate heat. Make patties of the rice mixture. Drop them into the oil and flatten each one with a spatula into a round. Lower heat to medium low and cook for 10 minutes on one side, 5 minutes on other side, and serve.

Easy Rice Croquettes

Croquettes go with everything. Serves 4.

2 lb (900 g) cooked rice
2 Tbs. Parmesan cheese, grated
1 tsp. parsley, chopped
1 clove of garlic, minced (optional)
pinch of basil
2–3 eggs
seasoned bread crumbs
oil for frying

In a large bowl mix together rice, cheese, parsley, garlic (if desired) and basil. Add 1 egg at a time until mixture sticks together. Wet hands in oil, shape rice into round croquettes. Roll croquettes in bread crumbs. Heat ¼ inch oil in a large pan. Fry a few at a time until golden brown all over. Drain on paper towels.

Alternatively, croquettes can be baked: place on a well-greased baking tray and bake at 350°F (180°C), mark 4, for about 30 minutes, or until golden brown. Serve with a tomato or cheese sauce.

Rice and Spinach Croquettes

These can be made and refrigerated in advance, then rolled in bread crumbs and fried before serving. Serves 4.

8 oz (225 g) cooked rice
8 oz (225 g) chopped cooked and drained spinach
3 eggs, beaten
1 tsp. salt
1 oz (25 g) Parmesan cheese, grated
pinch of basil
1 clove of garlic, minced
bread crumbs
oil for frying

Mix together rice, spinach, eggs, salt, cheese, basil and garlic. Form into small balls the size of golf balls. Roll in bread crumbs. Heat ½ inch oil in a large pan. Fry a few at a time until golden brown, about 3 minutes. Keep warm in oven until served.

Italian Rice Croquettes

More work than the last two recipes but very good!
Serves 4.

1 tsp. salt
1 lb 8 oz (675 g) cooked rice
1 Tbs. olive oil
1 small onion, chopped
1 medium carrot, chopped
1 stick of celery, chopped
2 oz (50 g) sliced mushrooms
2 medium tomatoes, peeled, seeded, and chopped
1 Tbs. tomato purée
12 fl oz (350 ml) vegetable stock or water
pinch of pepper
pinch of thyme
pinch of basil
1 Tbs. parsley, chopped
4 oz (125 g) mozzarella cheese, cut into 8 cubes
2 Tbs. flour
1 egg, beaten
bread crumbs
oil for frying

Heat olive oil in a medium saucepan; sauté onion,
carrots and celery until slightly brown. Add mushrooms
and sauté then add tomatoes and continue to cook until
they are soft. Add tomato purée, stock, salt, pepper and
spices; lower heat and cook for about 40 minutes. Add
rice to this mixture and mix well. Cool. Divide into 8
equal portions and shape into balls; place a piece of
cheese in the centre of each ball, roll in flour, dip in
egg and roll in bread crumbs. Deep fry in oil for about
2 minutes.

Brown Rice Quiche

Quiche might be passed up by many cooks as too time-consuming or difficult. This is usually because of the pastry. This is an easier method, using rice as the base. Here are two of my favourite brown rice quiches. Serves 4–6.

12 oz (350 g) cooked rice, pressed on to an oiled pie dish. If the rice is a little on the moist side, you might want to dry it out. Bake at 350°F (180°C), mark 4, for about 5 minutes. Or you can pour your favourite filling over the rice.

Cheese and Mushroom Filling

8 oz (225 g) Cheddar cheese, grated
3 eggs
8 oz (225 ml) milk
1 Tbs. wholewheat flour
½ tsp. salt
pinch of nutmeg (optional)
4 oz (125 g) mushrooms, sliced
1 small onion, chopped
1 Tbs. butter

Sauté mushrooms and onions in butter. Arrange evenly over rice base. Add flour to cheese and toss lightly, then add to rice base over mushroom mixture. Beat eggs with milk, salt and nutmeg; pour over all ingredients. Bake in oven, 350°F (180°C), mark 4, for 10 minutes. Reduce heat to 325°F (170°C) mark 3 and continue to bake 25–30 minutes or until filling puffs up golden and brown. For a plain quiche, omit mushrooms and onions.

Courgette Filling

1 small onion, chopped
2 tsp. tamari
3 eggs
4 oz (125 g) Cheddar cheese, grated
1 Tbs. butter
3 medium courgettes, diced
6 fl oz (175 ml) milk
1 tsp. salt
½ tsp. basil

Sauté onion in butter until soft. Add tamari and stir. Add courgettes and sauté for 2 minutes. Add about 2 Tbs. water and steam for 5 minutes. Courgettes should be half cooked. Beat together eggs, milk, cheese and seasonings. First pour courgette mixture into rice base, then pour over all the egg mixture. Bake at 350°F (180°C), mark 4, for 40 minutes or until eggs are set.

Rice Cheese Almond Casserole

An easy-to-assemble casserole. Serve with a salad and steamed carrots. Serves 4.

1 lb 8 oz (675 g) cooked rice
8 oz (225 g) Cheddar cheese, grated
½ tsp. salt
16 fl oz (450 ml) milk
3 eggs, lightly beaten
1 Tbs. melted butter
blanched slivered almonds

Preheat oven to 350°F (180°C), mark 4. Combine all the ingredients except the almonds. Turn into an oiled casserole dish. Top with almonds. Bake for 40 minutes or until set.

Swiss Brown
Rice

Cheddar cheese can be used instead of Gruyère or Emmental, or try a combination. Serves 4–6.

1 Tbs. oil
1 medium onion, sliced
3 sticks of celery, chopped
4 oz (125 g) mushrooms, sliced
4 Tbs. parsley, chopped
1 clove of garlic, minced
1 tsp. salt
¼ tsp. ground ginger
1 lb 8 oz (675 g) cooked rice
1 lb (450 g) Gruyère or Emmental cheese, grated

Heat a large pan. Add oil and sauté the onions, garlic, celery, mushrooms and parsley. Add salt, pepper and ginger. Layer the rice, vegetables and cheese in a shallow casserole dish. Repeat layers. Sprinkle with water before adding last layer of cheese. Bake 20–25 minutes in oven at 350°F (180°C), mark 4.

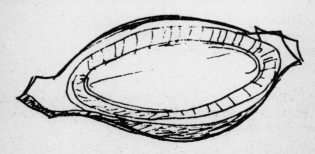

Baked Rice and Cheese

A nice change from macaroni and cheese. The topping is an added plus. Serves 4.

1 lb 8 oz (675 g) cooked rice
2 Tbs. butter
6 oz (275 g) Cheddar cheese, grated
16 fl oz (450 ml) milk
1 small onion, minced
1 egg

Mix together all ingredients; pour into an oiled baking dish. Bake at 350°F (180°C), mark 4, for about 50 minutes or until set and brown. Before serving, top with curry-flavoured toasted bread cubes.

Topping

2 Tbs. butter
½ tsp. curry powder
2 slices of bread, cut into cubes

Melt butter in a small pan, stir in curry, add bread cubes and brown lightly. These are also great tossed with noodles and butter.

Rice and Cheese Casserole

Serves 4

2 eggs, beaten
4 fl oz (125 ml) double cream
6 fl oz (75 ml) water
1 lb 8 oz (675 g) cooked rice
6 oz (175 g) Cheddar cheese, grated
1 tsp. salt
½ green pepper, chopped
1 small onion, chopped

Beat the eggs together with the cream and water. Add rice, cheese, salt, green pepper and onion. Mix well. Turn into an oiled casserole dish and bake at 350°F (180°C), mark 4, for 45 minutes or until set.

Onions - supply a small amount of vitamins 'a' and 'c'; calcium and phosphorus -

They are a good source of potassium and sulphur-

Rice Soufflé

Light and airy, this dish turns out perfect every time.
Serves 4.

6 oz (175 g) Cheddar cheese, grated
1 lb (450 g) cold cooked rice
1 Tbs. butter
1 Tbs. flour
8 fl oz (225 ml) milk
½ tsp. salt
¼ tsp. paprika
¾ tsp. curry powder
4 eggs, separated

Preheat oven to 350°F (180°C), mark 4. Melt the
butter in a saucepan and stir in the flour. Gradually add
milk and seasonings. Cook, stirring until thick. Add
cheese, cook until melted. Remove from heat. Add the
rice, mixing well. Mix a little of the hot mixture into the
egg yolks, return mixture with yolks to the saucepan,
stirring until mixture thickens. Cool. Beat the egg whites
stiff, then fold into cooled cheese and rice mixture. Bake
in a buttered casserole or soufflé dish for 40 minutes.

Curried Rice

Great served with steamed vegetables and a salad.
Serves 4.

16 fl oz (450 ml) water
8 oz (225 g) rice
8 oz (225 g) peeled and chopped tomatoes, fresh or tinned
1 small onion, chopped
½ green pepper, chopped
2 Tbs. butter
1½ tsp. curry powder
pinch of thyme
¾ tsp. salt

Sauté onion and green pepper in butter in a medium saucepan. Add curry powder, thyme and salt. Add rice, stirring for about 5 minutes. Add tomatoes and water, bring to a boil, cover and simmer for 50 minutes or until rice is tender.

German Curry

Every country has a favourite curry recipe. Serves 6.

1 lb (450 g) rice
2 tsp. salt
2 Tbs. butter
32 fl oz (900 ml) water
2 medium onions, sliced
1 Tbs. flour
1 Tbs. curry powder
24 fl oz (675 ml) water or vegetable stock
pepper to taste
4 fl oz (125 ml) double cream
1 Tbs. parsley, chopped

Bring water to a boil and add rice, salt and half the butter. Cover, lower heat to simmer and cook for about 50 minutes. Melt remaining butter in pan and sauté onions over low heat until soft. Add flour, curry powder, water, salt and pepper. Continue to cook until mixture becomes thick. Gradually add cream, stirring to heat through. Pour curry sauce over rice, sprinkle with chopped parsley and serve.

Curried Rice-and Peas

This dish has no salt. Curry powder makes a good seasoning in a salt-free diet. Serves 4.

1 medium onion, chopped
1 Tbs. butter
1 Tbs. curry powder
1 lb 8 oz (675 g) hot cooked rice
8 oz (225 g) peas, frozen or fresh

Melt butter in a medium saucepan; add curry powder and sauté onion over medium heat for 5 minutes. Add rice and peas, heat through and serve. A little water may be needed to prevent mixture sticking to pan, especially if using fresh peas.

To most Asian people rice is life itself.

Rice Walnut Loaf

Left-overs make a good sandwich spread. Serves 4.

1 small onion, chopped
½ green pepper, chopped
1 Tbs. oil or butter
8 oz (225 g) cooked rice
2 oz (50 g) bread crumbs
4 oz (125 g) tomatoes, chopped
2 oz (50 g) parsley, chopped
1 tsp. salt
pinch of dried sage

Sauté onion and green pepper in oil. Mix with rest of ingredients in a bowl. Place all ingredients in a greased baking dish. Bake at 375°F (190°C), mark 5, for about 30 minutes. Serve with tomato sauce.

Variation
After baking, cover the top with mashed potatoes and dot with butter. Brown under grill.

Carrot Rice Loaf

This is our favourite loaf recipe. Serve with tomato sauce, heated with a pinch of basil and a little garlic. Serves 4.

8 oz (225 g) carrots, grated
1 lb 8 oz (675 g) cooked rice
4 oz (125 g) peanuts, finely chopped
2 eggs
1 Tbs. oil
1 Tbs. green pepper, chopped
½ medium onion, chopped
1 tsp. dry mustard
1 Tbs. tamari

Grind the carrots and peanuts in a blender. Mix all ingredients, bake in an oiled casserole dish or loaf pan for about 1 hour at 350°F (180°C) mark 4.

Carrots - are high in potassium, calcium, iron, magnesium, manganese, sulphur, chlorine, phosphorus, and protein. They are also the best known source of vitamin 'A'

Rice Rings

A good dish for a buffet. Serves 4-6.

1 lb 8 oz (675 g) cooked rice
1 tsp. salt
1 clove of garlic, minced
2 oz (50 g) butter
pinch of sage
pinch of thyme
pinch of marjoram
1 medium onion, minced
2 oz (50 g) pine nuts

Melt butter and seasonings in a pan, sauté garlic, onions and pine nuts. Mix all ingredients and pour into a buttered 8 in (20 cm) ring mould. Set mould in a pan of hot water and bake for 20 minutes at 350°F (180°C), mark 4. To serve, loosen edges with a knife, invert on serving dish and fill with sautéed mushrooms.

Rice Carrot Ring

Another great dish for buffets. Serves 4-6.

3 large carrots, grated
1 small onion, minced
12 oz (350 g) cooked rice
1 egg, beaten
1 tsp. salt
4 oz (125 g) Parmesan cheese, grated
8 oz (225 g) cooked peas

Cook carrots for 3 minutes in boiling salted water. Drain thoroughly and add all the other ingredients. Turn into a buttered ring mould. Bake for 30 minutes at 350°F (180°C) mark 4. Unmould on plate and serve with peas in centre.

Veggie Rice
Casserole

Serves 4–6

2 fl oz (50 ml) oil
1 small onion, chopped
2 sticks of celery, chopped
2 carrots, diced
4 oz (125 g) mange-touts
4 oz (125 g) bean sprouts
4 oz (125 g) Chinese leaves
2 Tbs. sesame seeds
2 oz (50 g) finely chopped walnuts
½ tsp. salt
1 Tbs. tamari
2 lb (900 g) cooked rice
2 eggs, beaten

Heat the oil in a large heavy pan and sauté onion, celery and carrots. Add Chinese leaves and mange-touts. Cover and cook without liquid until wilted. Add bean sprouts, sesame seeds, walnuts, salt and tamari. Cover and steam for 3 minutes. Mix in rice and heat through. Make a well in the centre of the vegetable mixture and add the eggs. Cook, stirring, until eggs are cooked. Serve.

Rice Nut
and casserole

Simple, quick and crunchy. Serves 4.

1 lb (450 g) cooked rice
4 oz (125 g) Cheddar cheese, grated
4 oz (125 g) Gruyère or Emmental cheese, grated
1 tsp. salt
2 eggs
1 onion, chopped
2 oz (50 g) almonds, chopped
2 oz (50 g) walnuts chopped
1 oz (25 g) sunflower seeds

Mix all ingredients in a well-oiled casserole dish. Bake at 350°F (180°C), mark 4 for 35 minutes or until set and well browned.

Sunflower seeds were first cultivated by the American Indians
Sunflower seeds are rich in 'E' and 'B' vitamins, protein unsaturated fatty acids, phosphorus, calcium, iron, fluorine, iodine, potassium, magnesium and zinc —

Rice and Spinach Casserole

Great for a crowd. This dish can be prepared early in the day and refrigerated, then heated for 45 minutes or more. Serves 8–10.

1 lb (450 g) spinach
1 Tbs. butter
1 Tbs. flour
16 fl oz (450 ml) milk
2 oz (50 g) Parmesan cheese, grated
1 tsp. salt
3 lb (1.3 kg) cooked rice
1 oz (25 g) bread crumbs

Wash spinach well and place in large saucepan. Cover and cook over low heat until wilted. Drain and chop. Melt the butter, stir in flour and gradually blend in milk. Stir in vinegar. The mixture will curdle, but become smooth when stirred. Heat, stirring until mixture thickens, then add cheese and salt. Mix the spinach and rice into the sauce and pour into a buttered casserole dish. Sprinkle top with bread crumbs and bake at 325°F (170°C), mark 3, for 20 minutes or until hot.

Rice Spinach
Gratin

Another easy-to-prepare casserole. Serves 4.

2 lb (900 g) spinach, cooked and drained, or 1 lb 4 oz
   of frozen chopped spinach, thawed, cooked and well
   drained
4 oz (125 g) Cheddar cheese, grated
8 oz (225 g) cooked rice
1 Tbs. chopped parsley
1 tsp. salt
2 Tbs. tomato purée
2 Tbs. melted butter
4 Tbs. bread crumbs

Combine all ingredients except the bread crumbs
and half the butter and pour into an oiled casserole
dish. Combine bread crumbs and remaining butter;
sprinkle over the top of the casserole. Bake at 325°F
(170°C), mark 3, for 20 minutes.

Paupers

Rice Lunch

This dish is always changing. Use the vegetables you have on hand or try my favourite combination.
Serves 8.

1 medium onion, sliced
3 carrots, diced
2 sticks of celery, chopped
1 medium courgette, sliced
1 turnip, peeled and chopped
1 small green pepper, seeded and diced
1 – 2 tomatoes, peeled and chopped
4 fl oz (125 ml) boiling salted water
1 oz (25 g) almonds, chopped
2 lb (900 g) cold cooked rice
1 Tbs. tamari
salt to taste

   Place all vegetables with water in a saucepan; cover and simmer until carrots are tender, about 15 minutes. Stir in almonds. Add rice and tamari and stir to mix; heat through and serve.

Turnips are a good source of vitamin 'C', calcium, sodium, phosphorus, and potassium —

103

Rice *Hungarian* style With Green Beans

Serves 4

2 Tbs. oil
1 medium onion, chopped
2 Tbs. parsley, chopped
1 tsp. salt
1 tsp. paprika
1 lb (450 g) green beans, fresh or frozen and thawed,
    cut into 1 inch pieces
16 fl oz (450 ml) water
2 tsp. rice vinegar or other mild vinegar
4 fl oz (125 ml) sour cream
1 lb 8 oz (675 g) cooked rice

Heat oil in a pan; sauté onion until limp, stir in
parsley, paprika, salt and beans. Stir and cook for about
5 minutes. They shouldn't brown. Mix vinegar in water
and pour over beans. Cover and simmer for 15 minutes
or until beans are tender. Add rice and heat through.
Mix some of bean mixture into sour cream and slowly
pour it back into pot. Simmer for 2–4 minutes and
serve.

Cajun Delight

Serves 4

16 fl oz (450 ml) water
8 oz (225 g) uncooked rice
1 Tbs. oil
1 clove of garlic, minced
1 onion, chopped
1 green pepper, chopped
1 stick of celery, chopped
1 carrot, chopped
1–2 chilli peppers, de-seeded and finely chopped
4 oz (225 g) sliced mushrooms
8 fl oz (225 ml) home-made tomato sauce
½ tsp. salt
pinch of basil
Cheddar cheese, grated

Boil water, add rice, simmer for 50 minutes or until done. Heat oil in a pan, sauté the vegetables about 5 minutes, add tomato sauce, salt and basil and simmer for 5 minutes. Add cooked rice to vegetables, top with grated cheese, cover and cook until cheese is melted.

Rice And Veggies

Any combination of vegetables can be used for this dish, which is flavoured with a dill and yoghurt sauce. Serves 4-6.

1 large red onion, chopped
1 clove of garlic, chopped
2 oz (50 g) butter or oil
12 oz (350 g) uncooked rice
24 fl oz (675 ml) water or vegetable stock
4 oz (125 g) fresh peas
1 stick of celery, sliced
2 carrots, sliced
1 medium courgette, sliced

Sauce
8 fl oz (225 ml) yoghurt
1 Tbs. fresh dill, chopped, or 1 tsp. dried dill
1 Tbs. fresh parsley, chopped, or 1 tsp. dried parsley
1 Tbs. sesame seeds

For the sauce, stir together ingredients and refrigerate until needed. Sauté onion and garlic in butter until tender. Add rice and sauté until translucent, lower heat, add water, cover and cook for 30 minutes. Stir in vegetables and cook, covered, for 15 minutes or until rice is tender and liquid has been absorbed. Stir in yoghurt sauce, heat through on low heat stirring continually. Serve.

Rice and Peas

This delicious dish is a favourite with us. It can be served as a side dish or a main dish with a Mexican meal. Great with a spinach and mushroom salad. Serves 4.

2 Tbs. olive oil
1 medium onion, chopped
1 small tin of tomatoes, chopped
1 tsp. salt
1 bay leaf
pinch of dried basil
8 oz (225 g) fresh or frozen peas
1 lb 8 oz (675 g) hot cooked rice
2 Tbs. Parmesan cheese, grated

Heat olive oil in a saucepan; sauté onion with bay leaf and basil until tender. Add tomatoes and salt, stir in peas and simmer for about 10 minutes. Add hot cooked rice to sauce, turn off heat, sprinkle with grated cheese, stir to mix and serve.

Rice and Bean Burgers

Soya beans, chick peas or kidney beans can be used, or a combination. Serve as patties with a tomato sauce or on wholemeal baps. Serves 4.

8 oz (225 g) cooked, drained beans
8 oz (225 g) cooked rice
1 small onion, finely chopped
2 eggs, lightly beaten
1 tsp. salt
½ tsp. savory
1 clove of garlic, minced (optional)
¼ tsp. paprika
2 oz (50 g) wholewheat bread crumbs
2 Tbs. parsley, chopped
1 oz (25 g) wheat germ, or bread crumbs

Grind the beans, using the coarse blade of a meat grinder. Mix all ingredients except the wheat gern. Form into four burger patties. Roll in wheat germ. Put under grill until lightly browned or bake on a baking tray at 350°F (180°C) mark 4, for 35 minutes.

Nuts and Rice Burgers

These can be made in the morning and chilled until lunch or dinner. Serves 4.

8 oz (225 g) peanuts, ground in a blender
8 oz (225 g) walnuts, ground in a blender
8 oz (225 g) cooked rice
4 oz (125 g) mild Cheddar cheese, grated
1 egg
½ onion, chopped
1 tsp. salt
¼ tsp. chilli powder
1 oz (25 g) bread crumbs or wholewheat flour
2 Tbs. oil

Mix together all ingredients except bread crumbs and oil. Shape into patties; roll in bread crumbs. Chill. Fry in a hot pan.

Peanuts are well known for their high protein content and are a part of the legume family. Walnuts are also a great source of protein and iron.

Stuffed Vegetables
Company's Coming

One of the best ways I know to serve a meal for a crowd is to have several kinds of rice-stuffed vegetables, a large salad and rolls or breads. The guests can choose their own favourite vegetable or a combination. A nice variety might be: stuffed green courgettes, peppers, tomatoes, aubergines and maybe cabbage rolls. The vegetables can be stuffed in the morning and will serve 15-20 people. You'll need at least 7½ lb of cooked rice. This is best achieved by cooking in three batches the day before it is needed.

Rice Stuffed Green Peppers

Peppers can be stuffed individually with left-over rice – spanish, curry, sesame rice, etc. – and frozen until you have enough for an instant meal. Each one will have a different stuffing.

This is a basic recipe to which you can add your favourite seasonings. Serves 4.

4 large green peppers
2 Tbs. oil
1 small onion, chopped
1 stick of celery, chopped
2 oz (50 g) mushrooms, sliced (optional)
2 oz (50 g) Cheddar cheese, grated
1 lb (450 g) cooked rice
1 clove of garlic, minced (optional)
1 tsp. dried basil (optional)
salt to taste
1 small tin of tomatoes, chopped
2 Tbs. Parmesan cheese, grated (optional)

Cut tops off peppers, cut out ribs and seeds and discard. Parboil in boiling water for 3-4 minutes. Sauté onion, celery and mushrooms. Add all ingredients except Parmesan cheese. Stuff peppers, sprinkle with Parmesan cheese and bake at 350°F (180°C), mark 4, for 35-45 minutes in a baking dish with 1 in of hot water in the bottom.

Variation
To freeze peppers, place on a baking sheet until frozen then store in plastic bags. Cook as above for about one hour or more.

Rice Stuffed
Courgettes

12 medium courgettes
1 lb 8 oz (675 g) cold cooked rice
2 sticks of celery, chopped
½ medium green pepper, chopped
1 Tbs. butter
1 Tbs. oil
4 oz (125 g) Cheddar cheese, grated
2 Tbs. tomato purée
1 tsp. dried basil
1 tsp. salt

Cut courgettes in half and scoop out centres; chop up pulp. Heat butter and oil in pan, sauté onion, celery, green pepper and courgette pulp. Add tomato puree, basil, salt and rice. Turn heat as low as possible, stir for about 1 minute. Add cheese and stir. Stuff courgettes. Bake at 350°F (180°C), mark 4, in a shallow baking dish for 40 minutes or until all the vegetables are hot and tender.

Rice Stuffed Tomatoes

6 large tomatoes
1 lb (450 g) cold cooked rice
1 oz (25 g) pine nuts or chopped walnuts
1 clove of garlic, minced (optional)
1 tsp. dill
1 tsp. salt
4 fl oz (125 ml) sour cream

Hollow out the tomatoes with a small knife. Remove as much pulp as possible, being careful not to disturb the basic shape. Chop the tomato pulp and combine with all the other ingredients. Stuff the tomatoes. Bake in oven as for courgettes. While cooking, occasionally baste with the pan juices.

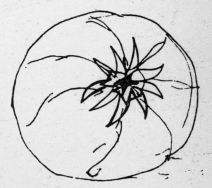

Rice Stuffed Aubergine

3 small aubergines
3 Tbs. chives, chopped
3 sticks of celery, chopped
2 Tbs. butter
2 oz (50 g) bean sprouts
1 lb 8 oz (675 g) cooked rice
2 Tbs. tamari

Cut aubergines in half lengthwise and scoop out centres, leaving a strong wall for stuffing. Chop pulp. Sauté onions, aubergine pulp and celery in butter. Add sprouts and stir. Add rice and tamari, stirring to distribute. Stuff aubergines. Bake as for courgettes.

Rice Stuffed Cabbage Rolls

Serves 6-8

2 Tbs. oil
1 medium onion, finely chopped
½ green pepper, chopped
1 tsp. salt
1 lb 8 oz (675 g) cooked rice
1 large can of sauerkraut
1 medium cabbage, steamed whole until leaves are limp, about 10 minutes, removing leaves as they become limp.
2 large tins of tomatoes, chopped

Sauté the onion and green pepper in oil until tender. Stir in rice, salt and sauerkraut. Spoon some of the filling on to each leaf; roll leaf around rice filling, tucking in sides. Place in an oiled glass baking dish; pour chopped tomatoes over all and bake at 350°F (180°C), mark 4, for 45 minutes.

Rice Stuffed Mushrooms

Mushrooms are a fungi, loaded with potassium, phosphorus, copper, and iron. They are also a good source of thiamine and riboflavin.

These stuffed mushrooms also make a sumptuous first course or side dish.

12 medium mushrooms
½ small onion, chopped
3 Tbs. butter
1 tsp. dried basil
½ tsp. salt
1 Tbs. Parmesan cheese, grated
4 oz (125 g) cold cooked rice

Melt 2 Tbs. butter in a small casserole dish. Remove stems from mushrooms, wash and dry the mushrooms and place them round side down in the dish. Chop stems very finely. Sauté onion and stems in rest of butter, combine with all ingredients. Fill mushrooms, making a mound in the centres. Bake at 350°F (180°C), mark 4, for 10-15 minutes or until rice stuffing is hot.

Saffron Rice

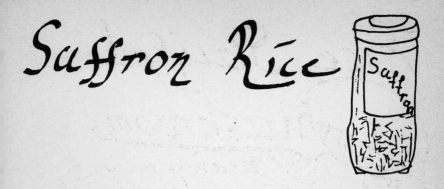

This is a superb dish to use as a base for curries or with steamed vegetables. Serves 4.

8 oz (225 g) uncooked rice
16 fl oz (450 ml) water
1 Tbs. lemon juice
½ tsp. saffron
½ tsp. salt
1 Tbs. butter

Bring water to a boil and add all ingredients. Lower heat and simmer for about 50 minutes, covered.

Chilli Rice

Terrific served as a side dish for a Mexican dinner or as a main course with any accompaniments. Serves 4.

1 medium onion, chopped
1 Tbs. butter
1 Tbs. tomato ketchup
2 tsp mustard
2 tsp. compound chilli seasoning
8 oz (225 g) uncooked rice
16 fl oz (450 ml) water

Sauté onion in butter, Add rice as for pilaf. Stir in the rest of the ingredients. Bring to a boil, cover and simmer for 50 minutes.

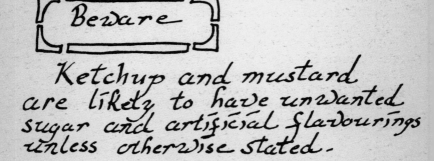

Beware

Ketchup and mustard are likely to have unwanted sugar and artificial flavourings unless otherwise stated.

Barbecued Rice Bean Dish

. . . .

Serves 8

1 lb (450 g) pinto or kidney beans
48 fl oz (1.3 l) water
3 large tins of tomatoes
2 tsp. salt
1 lb (450 g) uncooked rice
1 medium onion, chopped
1 green pepper, chopped
2 sticks of celery, chopped
2 fl oz (50 ml) molasses
1 Tbs. prepared mustard
1 tsp. salt
3-4 tsp. chilli powder

Wash beans. Place in a large pan, add water and bring to a boil. Boil for 2 minutes. Remove from heat and let stand for 1 hour. Cover and cook on low heat for about 2 hours or until tender. Drain beans, reserving liquid. Drain tomatoes, reserving liquid. Combine with water to make 32 fl oz (900 ml) of liquid to cook the rice in. Bring liquid to a boil with salt. Add rice, cover and simmer for about 50 minutes. Heat oil in a pan: sauté onion, green pepper and celery. Add to beans, along with rice and remaining ingredients in a large casserole dish. Bake at 350°F (180°C), mark 4, for 1 hour, stirring occasionally.

Mexican
Casserole

A good one-dish meal to serve with a salad. Serves 4–6.

1 Tbs. butter
2 Tbs. oil
12 oz (350 g) rice, soaked in salted water for at least
   30 minutes, then drained
¼ tsp. saffron
3 medium carrots, diced
1 large onion, peeled and quartered
8 oz (225 g) sweetcorn, fresh or frozen
4 oz (125 g) green peas, fresh or frozen
2 Tbs. tomato purée
24 fl oz (575 ml) soup stock or water
1 tsp salt
1 tsp. chilli powder

   Heat oil and butter in a saucepan; sauté carrots,
onions and celery. Then add the sweetcorn and peas.
Stir in rice, tomato purée, soup stock, saffron, salt and
chilli powder. Bring to a boil, cover and reduce heat.
Cook until liquid is absorbed, about 50 minutes. Fluff
with fork and serve.

Mexican Rice

Serves 4

2 Tbs. oil
1 Tbs. butter
8 oz (225 g) uncooked rice
1 large onion, chopped
1 green pepper, chopped
1 small tin of tomatoes,
   chopped
1 tsp. salt
1 tsp. chilli powder
½ tsp. dry mustard
pinch of cumin
3 oz (75 g) Cheddar cheese,
   grated

Heat oil and butter in a medium saucepan; sauté onion and green pepper. Add rice and stir until rice is coated with the oil and butter. Add water to tomato sauce to make 16 fl oz (450 ml). Add all of the ingredients to the rice, except cheese. Stir, cover and simmer for about 50 minutes. Transfer rice to serving dish and stir in cheese.

Oriental Dishes
Basic Stir Fry

We have a stir-fry at least once a week. This is one dish that is always changing and can be as seasonal as the vegetables you buy.

While the rice is cooking, I chop and slice vegetables – onions, green peppers, carrots, courgettes, tomatoes, mushrooms, broccoli, celery, or whatever I have available.

When the rice is done, I leave it covered on the burner and sauté the vegetables in hot oil with minced garlic. When they are cooked, I add bean sprouts, peas or mange-touts and heat them through. Then I stir in a tamari sauce, made with 6 fl oz (175 ml) water, 1–3 tsp. arrowroot or cornflour, a pinch of dried ginger and 1 Tbs. tamari. Stir to blend in arrowroot and pour over vegetables, stirring until thickened. Serve up rice on plates and cover with vegetables. Additional tamari can be added if desired.

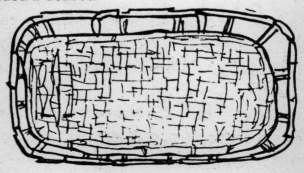

Fried Rice with Almonds

Serve as a dish with stir-fried vegetables. Serves 4.

1 small onion, chopped
2 sticks of celery, chopped
3 Tbs. oil
1 lb 8 oz (675 g) cold cooked rice
1–2 Tbs. tamari
2 oz (50 g) slivered almonds

Sauté onions and celery in oil. Add and fry rice. If too dry, add more oil. Stir in tamari, coating rice thoroughly. Add almonds and serve.

The Chinese have been eating rice longer than the Japanese, by a few thousand years.

Rice is consumed at every meal, except in North China.

Chinese Fried Rice

Serve a green salad with mandarin oranges and a creamy dressing. Serves 4.

1 large onion, chopped
2 sticks of celery, chopped
1 small green pepper, chopped
3 Tbs. oil
2 eggs, beaten
1 lb 8 oz (675 g) cold cooked rice
2 green onions, chopped
8 oz (225 g) peas, fresh or frozen
2 Tbs. tamari

Heat oil in a pan or wok and sauté onion, celery and green pepper. Add the eggs, stirring and breaking them up as they cook. Stir in rice, green onions and peas. Lower heat and add tamari; mix well. If rice sticks, add more tamari or oil. When heated through, serve.

Tamari is a natural soy sauce fermented for at least two years in wooden casks. Tamari is made from wheat, sea salt, and soy beans—

Brown Rice *Oriental*

(Style)

Serves 4-6

3 Tbs. oil
1 medium onion, chopped
1 clove of garlic, minced
3 sticks of celery, chopped
1 small tin of water chestnuts, sliced
8 oz (225 g) bean sprouts
½ tsp. basil
1 Tbs. fresh ginger, grated
2 fl oz (50 ml) honey
2 fl oz (50 ml) tamari
2 Tbs. lemon juice
2 lb (900 g) cooked brown rice

In a heavy pan or wok, heat the oil, and sauté onion, celery and garlic. Add water chestnuts and bean sprouts; stir and cook for 1 minute. Stir in basil. Combine honey, tamari, grated ginger and lemon juice; stir into the vegetables. Add the cooked rice. Heat through and serve.

Ginger - a stimulant - promotes cleansing through perspiration - also good for colic and to stimulate flow of saliva -

Originally from Southeast Asia, ginger is grown in southern China and Japan -

125

Chow Mein

Another version of a stir-fry. Serves 4.

2 Tbs. oil
1 medium onion, chopped
1–2 tsp. fresh ginger, grated
2 carrots, sliced thin
2 sticks of celery, chopped
4 oz (225 g) mushrooms, sliced
4 oz (225 g) mange-touts
4 oz (225 g) bean sprouts
8 fl oz (225 ml) water
1 Tbs. tamari
2 Tbs. sherry (optional)
1 Tbs. arrowroot

While the rice is cooking, prepare the vegetables. When the rice is ready, heat the oil in a heavy pan or wok and sauté the vegetables. Scoop the vegetables out of the pan and set them aside. Put the water, tamari and sherry in pan and bring to a boil. Dissolve the arrowroot in a little water and slowly stir into the boiling mixture. Stir until mixture thickens. Return the stir-fried vegetables to the sauce to re-heat them. Serve over cooked rice.

Sweet and Sour

Sauce with Vegetables over Rice

Serves 4

Sauce
1 small tin of tomatoes, chopped
2 fl oz (50 ml) rice vinegar
½ tsp. curry powder
¼ tsp. chilli powder
2 Tbs. tamari
½ tsp. dry mustard
2 tsp. honey or to taste
1 tsp. arrowroot

Vegetables
3 carrots, sliced diagonally
3 sticks of celery, sliced diagonally
1 medium green pepper, sliced in strips
A few spring onions, chopped
1 small tin of water chestnuts, sliced
1 small tin of bamboo shoots
2 Tbs. oil

Combine all ingredients for sauce. Put on side. Heat oil
in a pan or wok; sauté green onions, carrots, celery and
green pepper. While vegetables are still crisp, add
water chestnuts and bamboo shoots; stir to heat
through. Stir in sauce, heat, and serve over rice.

A Japanese cold vinegared rice. Serves 4–6.

1 lb (450 g) uncooked rice
32 fl oz (900 ml) water
1 3 in-piece of kombu (seaweed), washed (optional)
2 fl oz (50 ml) rice vinegar
1 fl oz (25 ml) honey
1 tsp. salt
pinch of dried ginger

Bring water to a boil, add rice and kombu. Cover and simmer for about 50 minutes. Discard kombu and let rice cool for a few minutes in a shallow pan. Mix vinegar, honey, salt and ginger. Pour over rice; mix and cool. Rice is ready to be used when it has reached room temperature.

A farmer says to me,
'You cannot live on vegetable
food solely, for it furnishes
nothing to make bones with,'
            and so he religiously
devotes a part of his day to
supplying his system with the
raw materials of bones.
            Walking all the while
he talks behind his oxen, which,
with vegetable made bones, jerks
him and his lumbering plough
in spite of every
            Obstacle

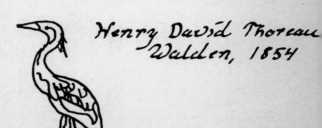

Henry David Thoreau
Walden, 1854

Desserts

A dessert should be enjoyed as a healthy treat. It should look good and taste delicious.

Sauces

Most of the rice custards and puddings for which recipes are given taste even better with one of these sauces. Or simply add to plain boiled rice.

Easy Honey Orange Sauce

4 fl oz (125 ml) honey
6 fl oz (375 ml) fresh orange juice
1 tsp. grated orange rind

Mix ingredients together. Chill.

Hot Orange Sauce

1 Tbs. butter
1 Tbs. flour
8 fl oz (225 ml) fresh orange juice
1 Tbs. apple juice concentrate
pinch of salt

Place butter in saucepan. Mix in flour, stirring over medium heat for 2 minutes. Add orange juice and apple juice concentrate and bring to a boil. Simmer until thick and creamy. Add salt. Remove from heat, serve or let cool.

Apricot Sauce

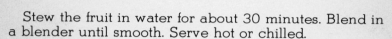

8 oz (225 g) dried apricots
12 fl oz (350 ml) water
1 Tbs. honey

Stew the fruit in water for about 30 minutes. Blend in a blender until smooth. Serve hot or chilled.

Hot Lemon Dessert Sauce

8 fl oz (225 ml) boiling water
3 fl oz (75 ml) honey
1 Tbs. arrowroot powder dissolved in a little water
1 Tbs. butter
2-3 Tbs. lemon juice

Simmer honey and arrowroot in boiling water until honey is dissolved. Add the rest of ingredients. Continue to simmer, stirring until thickened.

Apple or Pear Sauce

3 apples or pears, peeled, cored and finely chopped
4-6 fl oz (125-75 ml) honey
1 Tbs. butter
1 Tbs. lemon juice
pinch of cinnamon
pinch of nutmeg

Combine all ingredients in a small saucepan and simmer until fruit is tender. Mash or blend. Serve hot or chilled.

Banana Sauce

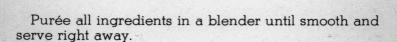

4 ripe bananas
1 orange, peeled
juice of 1 lemon
2 fl oz (50 ml) water
pinch of cinnamon

Purée all ingredients in a blender until smooth and
serve right away.

Bananas have calcium, iron, phosphorus, and vitamins 'A' and 'C' and are a terrific source of potassium-

Zippy Rice Pudding

Assemble and serve or chill. Great for unexpected guests or a quick lunch. Serves 6.

2 oz (50 g) raisins
1 lb 8 oz (675 g) cold cooked rice
2 fl oz (50 ml) honey
2 oz (50 ml) walnuts, coarsely chopped
16 fl oz (450 ml) plain yoghurt
½ tsp. cinnamon
juice of 1 lemon

Mix all ingredients.

Traditional Rice Pudding

Long-cooking old-fashioned pudding. Serves 4.

2 oz (50 g) uncooked rice
½ tsp. salt
1 Tbs. honey
½ tsp. cinnamon
¼ tsp nutmeg
1 tsp. vanilla essence
8 fl oz (225 g) water
8 fl oz (225 g) milk
1 egg

Combine rice, salt, honey, cinnamon, nutmeg and vanilla in water. Bring to a boil, cover, reduce heat and simmer for 1 hour. In the top of a double boiler, beat the milk and egg together. Pouring very slowly, gradually stir rice mixture into the egg and milk, making sure it does not curdle. Cook in the top of the double boiler over hot water, simmering for about 1 hour or until set. Serve warm or cold.

Molasses Rice Pudding

Iron-rich molasses gives this pudding a rich flavour. Serves 4.

2 eggs, beaten
½ tsp. salt
3 fl oz (75 g) molasses
8 oz (225 g) cooked rice
grated peel of 1 lemon
juice of 1 lemon
½ tsp. cinnamon
¼ tsp. nutmeg

Mix together the beaten eggs, salt, milk and molasses. Add the cooked rice and the rest of the ingredients. Stir well. Pour mixture into an oiled casserole dish. Bake for 1 hour at 350°F (180°C), mark 4.

Walnut Currant Rice Pudding

Serves 4

1 lb (450 g) cooked rice
8 fl oz (225 ml) cream
2 eggs, beaten
3 oz (75 g) walnuts, chopped
2 oz (50 g) currants or raisins
1 tsp. cinnamon
¼ tsp. nutmeg
¼ tsp. cloves
1 tsp. vanilla essence

Combine all ingredients. Pour into a buttered baking dish. Bake for about 25 minutes at 375°F (190°C), mark 5.

Creamy Rice Custard

A special dessert when you have guests. The citrus flavours are great after a spicy meal. Serves 6.

24 fl oz (675 ml) milk
4 oz (125 g) uncooked rice
1 tsp salt
2 fl oz (50 ml) honey
2 eggs, separated
6 fl oz (175 ml) cream
1 tsp. vanilla essence
1 Tbs. orange peel
1 Tbs. lemon peel

Combine first 4 ingredients. Cook, covered, in a double boiler until rice is soft, about 1 hour. Beat egg yolks and cream; add a small amount of the rice mixture to this. Slowly pour the egg and cream mixture into rice, cooking, covered, until thick, about 20 minutes. Stir occasionally. Remove from heat, add vanilla and peel. Cool slightly. Beat egg whites until stiff and fold into custard. Chill. Serve in individual dishes.

Old Fashioned Rice Pudding

This pudding doesn't use a sweetener. The vanilla and cinnamon bring out the sweetness of the rice. Serves 4.

4 oz (125 g) uncooked rice
16 fl oz (450 ml) water
2 eggs, beaten
24 fl oz (675 ml) milk
1 Tbs. butter
pinch of salt
½ tsp. cinnamon
1 tsp. vanilla essence

Boil the rice in the water for 5 minutes, then drain. Combine eggs and milk, add rice and the rest of ingredients and pour into a buttered casserole dish. Bake at 325°F (170°C), mark 3, uncovered, for 1½ hours or until set. Cool and serve at room temperature with a fruit sauce.

Pineapple Rice

A heavenly treat – pineapple and whipped cream.
Serves 4–6.

2 oz (50 g) uncooked rice
16 fl oz (450 ml) milk
1 fl oz (25 ml) honey
pinch of salt
1 tsp. vanilla essence
¼ tsp. nutmeg
2 fl oz (50 ml) milk
4 fl oz (125 ml) double cream, whipped
1 small tin of crushed pineapple, drained

In a saucepan over low heat cook rice, milk, honey
and salt. Stir occasionally to prevent sticking until rice
is tender, 40–50 minutes. Remove from heat. Stir in
nutmeg, vanilla and milk. Refrigerate until well chilled.
Fold in whipped cream and pineapple before serving.

Baked Rice With Dates

Make this recipe on a lazy
afternoon and serve with
whipped cream. Serves 4.

32 fl oz (900 ml) milk
4 oz (125 g) uncooked rice
2 fl oz (50 ml) honey
pinch of salt
2 oz (50 g) dates, chopped
whipped cream

Mix all the ingredients except for the cream in a
buttered casserole dish. Bake at 300°F (150°C), mark 2
until a light brown skin forms over the surface. Stir the
skin into the pudding and cook until another skin forms
and stir that in too. Continue to do so for two or more
hours. Then bake, without stirring, until rice is tender
and top is well browned. Cool and serve with whipped
cream.

Dates have been cultivated
in the Middle East since
3000 B.C. and in California as
late as 1958. Dates need to
be grown where the summers
are hot and dry and near
a water supply as they need
constant irrigation.

Rice and Currant Pudding

Serves 4

24 fl oz (675 ml) milk
3 eggs, lightly beaten
1 tsp. vanilla essence
2 fl oz (50 ml) honey
½ tsp. salt
1 lb (450 g) cooked rice
2 oz (50 g) walnuts or other nuts, chopped
3 oz (75 g) currants
pinch of nutmeg
½ tsp. cinnamon

Beat the milk, eggs, vanilla, honey and salt together. Add rice, currants, nutmeg and cinnamon. Turn into a buttered casserole dish and bake at 350°F (180°C), mark 4, for 30 minutes or until pudding is the desired consistency. The pudding might become dry if baked too long.

Currants were probably first cultivated a little before 1600 in Denmark and the Netherlands.

Baked Rice Pudding

The subtle flavour of lemon is a nice addition to this pudding. Serves 4.

1 lb (450 g) cooked rice
3 oz (75 g) raisins
1 Tbs. grated lemon peel
2 tsp. lemon juice
3 fl oz (75 ml) honey
1 tsp. vanilla essence
3 eggs
½ tsp. salt
pinch of nutmeg

Place the rice, raisins, peel and juice in a buttered baking dish. Beat together remaining ingredients except nutmeg and pour over rice; stir to mix. Sprinkle with nutmeg. Bake at 325°F (170°C), mark 3, for 30 minutes or until set.

Dessert Rice Pancakes

After a light dinner, serve these with warm honey, apple sauce or a fruit sauce. Serves 4.

8 oz (225 g) cooked rice
1 oz (25 g) raisins (optional)
2 oz (50 g) almonds, chopped
3 fl oz (75 ml) milk
1 egg
1–2 Tbs. honey
butter to fry

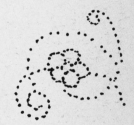

In a covered saucepan over a low heat simmer rice, raisins and almonds in milk until liquid is absorbed. Remove from heat and stir in egg and honey. More milk might need to be added if mixture is too dry. Heat butter in a pan. Drop mixture by tablespoonfuls and flatten a little. Brown lightly on both sides and serve.

Rice 'N' Fruit

No cooking makes this
an easy dessert. Serves 4.

1 lb (450 g) cold cooked rice
2 oz (50 g) dates, chopped
1 Tbs. honey
½ tsp. cinnamon
2 oz (50 g) walnuts or almonds, chopped
1 small tin of crushed pineapple
whipped cream
fresh strawberries, raspberries or other soft fruit, if
    available

Combine the rice, dates, honey, cinnamon, nuts and
pineapple. Chill thoroughly. Serve topped with whipped
cream and soft fruit.

Coconut Rice Cake

This is an easy and nutritious dessert. Serves 6–8.

12 oz (350 g) rice
35 fl oz (1 l) water
2 fl oz (50 ml) honey
pinch of nutmeg
½ tsp. vanilla essence
1 tsp. cinnamon
2 oz (50 g) butter, softened
2 oz (50 g) sesame seeds (optional)
salt to taste
4 oz (125 g) coconut, grated

Boil rice in the water for about 30 minutes or until very soft. Drain. Combine the rest of ingredients, pressing into a shallow baking pan at least 10 in (25 cm) in diameter and cool. Cut into squares and serve like cake. Great topped with Hot Lemon Dessert Sauce.

Rice Dessert Balls

For a change, serve these topped with strawberries and yoghurt instead of sour cream. Serves 4.

8 oz (225 g) uncooked rice
16 fl oz (450 ml) milk
2 fl oz (50 ml) honey
2 tsp. grated lemon peel
juice of ½ lemon
½ tsp. salt
1 Tbs. butter
vanilla essence to taste
2 fl oz (50 ml) sour cream
cinnamon
nutmeg

Cook rice in milk sweetened with honey in a covered saucepan over low heat until cooked, about 50 minutes. Mix with remaining ingredients except sour cream, cinnamon and nutmeg. Form rice mixture into balls the size of walnuts. Chill. Serve topped with sour cream and sprinkled with cinnamon and nutmeg.

Apple Cinnamon Rice Fritters

Also great for breakfast, brunch or lunch. Serves 4.

1 egg, beaten
1 lb (450 g) cold cooked rice
8 oz (225 g) apples chopped
3 oz (75 g) honey
1 tsp. cinnamon
¼ tsp. nutmeg
1 tsp. lemon peel
oil for frying

Combine all the ingredients, except the oil. Form into small flat oval cakes. Pour oil into a pan, one inch deep, and heat. Carefully drop the cakes into the oil. Fry a few at a time. Keep warm until all are fried. Add a little honey to serve.

Rice Custard

Serves 4

3 oz (75 g) cooked rice
16 fl oz (450 ml) milk
3 oz (75 g) cooked rice
2 eggs
2 oz (75 g) honey
1 tsp. vanilla essence
½ tsp. cinnamon
¼ tsp. nutmeg
2 oz (50 g) raisins (optional)

Combine all ingredients. Pour into oiled custard cups or a baking dish. Sprinkle with additional nutmeg. Bake at 325°F (170°C), mark 3, for about 1 hour or until a knife inserted in centre comes out clean.

INDEX

151